What Should I Do?
Social and Moral Scenarios for Ages 4-7

Big Choices for Little Hearts

By: Amanda Aliff, LPC, NCC, CCTP

Copyright © 2025 by Amanda Aliff, LPC, NCC, CCTP

All rights reserved. No part of this book may be reproduced or transmitted in any form or by any means, electronic or mechanical, including photocopying, recording, or by any information storage and retrieval system, without permission in writing from the copyright owner. This book was printed in the United States of America.

ISBN-13: 978-1-961752-31-3 (Paperback)
ISBN-13: 978-1-961752-32-0 (Hardback)
ISBN-13: 978-1-961752-33-7 (Kindle)

For my amazing children,

You have been my greatest guides on this journey of parenthood.

Through your curiosity, kindness, and boundless energy,

You have taught me what it truly means to grow, learn, and love unconditionally.

With love always.

Table of Contents

Letter for Parents and Caregivers..6

Introduction..8

Stick Figure Seek-and-Find Challenge...................................11

Chapter 1: Friendship and Social Skills....................................12

Chapter 2: School and Learning...17

Chapter 3: Family and Home Life..22

Chapter 4: Community and Kindness......................................27

Chapter 5: Decision-Making and Ethics.................................33

Chapter 6: Environmental Responsibility..............................38

Chapter 7: Technology and Media..45

Chapter 8: Emotional Challenges..52

Chapter 9: Health and Safety...59

Chapter 10: Cultural Awareness...66

Chapter 11: Teamwork and Cooperation................................72

Chapter 12: Imagination and Creativity....................................79

Chapter 13: Responsibility and Independence.......................86

Chapter 14: Facing Challenges...92

Chapter 15: Becoming Your Best Self....................................100

Bonus Questions..103

Dear Parents and Caregivers,

Welcome to this special journey of teaching and guiding your child through important life skills, values, and decision-making! This book is designed to encourage meaningful conversations between you and your child, using relatable scenarios and thought-provoking questions tailored for their age.

As you explore the book together, you may notice that there is not always one "right" answer to the questions. In fact, the beauty of this approach lies in its flexibility—many scenarios offer multiple possible answers, each reflecting different perspectives, values, or approaches to problem-solving. The goal is not to arrive at a single solution but to inspire curiosity, self-reflection, and open dialogue.

Here are some tips to make the most of this book:
1. **Encourage Open Discussion**: Use the scenarios and questions as conversation starters. Ask your child why they chose a particular answer and how they might feel in that situation. This helps develop empathy and critical thinking.
2. **Explore Multiple Answers**: Discuss how different choices could lead to different outcomes. This will show your child that there are often many ways to handle a situation, and all choices have consequences.
3. **Share Your Own Experiences**: Whenever possible, share stories from your life that connect to the scenarios. Your experiences can help your child see how these lessons apply to the real world.

4. **Focus on Growth, Not Perfection**: Remind your child that it is okay to make mistakes. The important part is learning from those experiences and continuing to grow.
5. **Celebrate Their Insights**: Acknowledge and praise your child for their thoughts and contributions. This builds their confidence and shows them that their voice matters.

Finally, this book is a tool to foster communication, understanding, and shared values between you and your child. By discussing these scenarios together, you are building a foundation of trust and helping your child navigate the complexities of life with kindness, confidence, and courage.

Thank you for being an essential part of your child's learning journey. Let us start these conversations and watch them grow into thoughtful, compassionate individuals!

Warm regards,
Amanda

Introduction: Welcome to "What Should I Do?"

Hello there, little thinker!

Every day, you make choices—some are simple, like picking which game to play, and others can be a little tricky, like deciding whether to share your toys or say "sorry" when you have hurt someone's feelings. This book is here to help you with those tricky choices!

Inside this book, you will find situations about children just like you. These children are figuring out what to do in different situations—at school, at home, with friends, and even at the playground. Each story will help you think about what you might do if you were in their place. You will also learn how your choices can make a big difference in how you feel and how others feel too!

Why This Book Was Made

This book was made just for children like you who want to:
- Be kind and helpful to others.
- Make smart and thoughtful choices.
- Learn how to do the right thing, even when it is hard.

Everyone makes mistakes sometimes, and that is okay! Mistakes help us learn. What is important is that we always try our best and think about how we can make good choices.

How to Use This Book

Here is how it works:
1. **Listen to the Tale:** Each example is about a situation you might face someday.
2. **Think About the Questions:** After each story, you will find questions to help you think about what you might do and how it feels.
3. **Talk About It:** Share your answers with a grown-up, teacher, or friend. Talking about your ideas can help you learn even more.

There is no one "perfect" answer to every situation, but if you think carefully and choose kindness and honesty, you will be on the right path.

Are you ready to start? Let us learn how to be thoughtful, kind, and brave—one choice at a time!

Stick Figure Seek-and-Find Challenge!

Hey there, awesome reader!

Are you ready for a fun challenge while you read this book?

Throughout these pages, 40 silly stick figures are hiding—and they are doing all kinds of goofy things! You might find one dancing, another doing a handstand, or even one wearing wacky sunglasses.

Your mission (if you choose to accept it):
Look carefully on each page and try to spot as many stick figures as you can.

But wait—there is more!
- Can you count how many stick figures you find?
- Which one is your favorite?
- What is the funniest thing a stick figure is doing?

When you have found all 40, give yourself a big high five—you are a Stick Figure Seek-and-Find Champion!

So get ready to giggle, and keep your eyes open. The stick figures cannot wait for you to find them!

Chapter 1

Friendship and Social Skills

Sharing a Toy

You bring a toy train to school, and a friend asks if they can play with it. You are not sure if they will be careful. Should you:
1. Say, "Let's play together!" so you can both enjoy it.
2. Say, "No, it's mine," and walk away.
3. Let them play alone and hope they take good care of it.

Explanation: Sharing and playing together builds trust and friendship. You can teach your friend how to take care of your toy while playing. Even though it can be hard to share something you love, it can make playtime more fun for everyone.

Follow-Up Questions:
- How do you feel when someone shares with you?
- What is something fun you can do together with the toy?
- Why is sharing a good way to make friends?

Including Others

You are building a tower with blocks, and another child is watching you. Should you:
1. Invite them to help you build the tower.
2. Ignore them and keep building on your own.
3. Tell them they cannot play with you because it is your project.

Explanation: Including others helps everyone feel happy and makes playtime more exciting. Working together also means you can build something even better than you could on your own!

Follow-Up Questions:
- How do you feel when someone asks you to join in?
- What are some ways you can make others feel included?
- Why is teamwork important when playing?

Saying Sorry

You accidentally bump into a friend and knock over their art project. Should you:
1. Say sorry and help them fix it.
2. Pretend it did not happen and walk away.
3. Blame someone else for the accident.

Explanation: Saying sorry and helping shows you care about your friend's feelings. Everyone makes mistakes, but being kind can make things better.

Follow-Up Questions:
- How do you feel when someone says sorry to you?
- What can you do to make things right when you hurt someone?
- Why is it important to be honest about accidents?

Taking Turns

You and your friend both want to use the same swing on the playground. Should you:
1. Take turns so you can both enjoy the swing.
2. Argue until the other person gives up.
3. Run and grab the swing first so you do not miss out.

Explanation: Taking turns is a fair way to share something fun. It also shows that you respect your friend and helps everyone have a good time.

Follow-Up Questions:
- How do you feel when someone lets you have a turn?
- What are some fun things you can do while waiting for your turn?
- Why is it important to be patient with friends?

Meeting a New Friend

A new classmate joins your group for story time. They look shy and do not say anything. Should you:
1. Smile and ask them to sit next to you.
2. Wait for someone else to talk to them.
3. Ignore them and keep talking with your other friends.

Explanation: Smiling and being welcoming can help someone new feel less nervous. It is a great way to make a new friend.

Follow-Up Questions:
- How do you feel when someone is kind to you?
- What can you say to make someone feel welcome?
- Why is it fun to make new friends?

Conclusion: Friendship means helping others feel happy, included, and cared for. Whether it is sharing toys, solving problems, or inviting someone new to join, every small action shows what a great friend you are.

When you make kind choices and think about how others feel, you build strong friendships. Let us practice being kind and brave, and remember: great friends make great choices!

Chapter 2

School and Learning

Asking for Help

You are trying to color inside the lines on a school worksheet, but it is hard, and you are getting frustrated. Should you:
1. Raise your hand and ask your teacher for help.
2. Scribble all over the page because it is too hard.
3. Sit quietly and not finish the worksheet.

Explanation: Asking for help is a good way to learn and get better at something. Everyone needs help sometimes, and your teacher is there to support you!

Follow-Up Questions:
- How do you feel when someone helps you?
- Why is it okay to ask for help when you are stuck?
- What can you do next time something feels hard?

Listening During Storytime

Your teacher is reading a story to the class, but your friend keeps whispering to you. Should you:
1. Focus on the story and let your friend know you will talk later.
2. Whisper back so your friend does not feel left out.
3. Keep looking at your friend and ignore the story.

Explanation: Paying attention during story time helps you enjoy the story and learn new things. It also shows respect for your teacher and classmates.

Follow-Up Questions:
- How do you feel when others listen to you?
- Why is it important to pay attention in class?
- What is your favorite part of listening to stories?

Taking Care of Your Supplies

You see a classmate left markers uncapped on the table after art time. Should you:
1. Cap the markers and put them away neatly.
2. Leave them there because it is not your mess.
3. Tell your teacher and ask them what to do.

Explanation: Taking care of supplies, even if they are not yours, helps everyone in the class. Being helpful keeps things organized.

Follow-Up Questions:
- Why is it important to clean up after yourself?
- How do you feel when you see a neat classroom?
- What are some ways you can help keep things organized?

Following the Teacher's Instructions

Your teacher asks the class to line up quietly to go outside for recess. You feel excited and want to run to the front of the line. Should you:
1. Wait patiently and follow the teacher's directions.
2. Push ahead of others to get to the front.
3. Keep talking to your friends and forget to line up.

Explanation: Following your teacher's instructions keeps everyone safe and helps the class run smoothly. Being patient and waiting your turn shows good listening skills.

Follow-Up Questions:
- How do you feel when everyone listens and works together?
- Why is it important to follow the rules in school?
- What can you do if you feel too excited to wait?

Trying Something New

Your teacher asks the class to try writing their names for the first time. You have never done it before and feel nervous. Should you:
1. Try your best and see how it turns out.
2. Say you cannot do it and not even try.
3. Scribble quickly and hope no one notices.

Explanation: Trying something new can feel hard, but it is the best way to learn! Even if it is not perfect, giving your best effort shows courage and helps you improve.

Follow-Up Questions:
- How do you feel when you try something new?
- Why is it okay to make mistakes while learning?
- What is something new you have learned to do recently?

Conclusion: School is a place where you can grow, learn, and have fun with your friends. Every day brings new challenges, whether it is solving a tricky problem, working with others, or trying something you have never done before. By being curious, patient, and open to learning, you can discover amazing things about the world—and yourself!

Remember, making mistakes is part of the learning process. Each time you try again, you get closer to success. Asking for help, sharing with others, and taking your time to do your best work are all ways to show that you are ready to learn and grow.

Keep exploring, stay curious, and do not be afraid to try new things. When you believe in yourself and work hard, there is no limit to what you can achieve. School is just the beginning of your big adventure in learning!

Chapter 3

Family and Home Life

Sharing Toys at Home

Your sibling wants to borrow your favorite puzzle, but you are worried they might lose a piece. Should you:
1. Help them put it together so you can watch over the pieces.
2. Say no and keep it for yourself.
3. Let them borrow it and hope for the best.

Explanation: Sharing with your siblings or family members helps everyone feel happy and loved. Taking turns teaches kindness and patience.

Follow-Up Questions:
- How do you feel when someone shares with you?
- What can you do if you are not ready to share right away?
- Why is sharing important in a family?

Helping with Dinner

Your parent is making dinner, and they ask if you would like to help set the table. You are watching your favorite cartoon. Should you:
1. Pause the show and help set the table.
2. Say no and keep watching.
3. Help after the cartoon is over without telling your parent.

Explanation: Helping at home is a great way to show your family you care. It does not take long and makes dinner more special for everyone.

Follow-Up Questions:
- How do you feel when someone helps you?
- What is your favorite way to help at home?
- Why is helping important in a family?

Cleaning Up After Playtime

You have been playing with your toys all afternoon, and now they are spread out across the living room. Your parent asks you to clean them up before dinner. Should you:
1. Start cleaning up right away.
2. Say you will clean up later but forget to do it.
3. Ask your parent to clean up with you so it is faster.

Explanation: Cleaning up after yourself shows responsibility and helps keep your home neat and organized. It is also a way to show respect.

Follow-Up Questions:
- How does a clean home make everyone feel?
- What is a fun way to make cleaning up easier?
- Why is it important to take care of your toys and space?

Saying Sorry After an Argument

You and your sibling both want to play with the same toy, and you yell at them. Should you:
1. Say sorry and take turns with the toy.
2. Stay mad and refuse to apologize.
3. Leave the room and hope they forget about the argument.

Explanation: Saying sorry when you have made a mistake shows that you care about your family's feelings. It helps you get along better and keeps everyone happy.

Follow-Up Questions:
- How do you feel when someone says sorry to you?
- Why is it important to apologize when you are wrong?
- What can you do to make things better after an argument?

Taking Care of Your Pet

Your pet looks sad and lonely while you are watching TV. Should you:
1. Stop and play with them for a little while.
2. Keep watching your show and ignore them.
3. Ask someone else to play with the pet instead.

Explanation: Pets need attention and love just like people do. Spending time with them helps them feel happy and cared for.

Follow-Up Questions:
- How do you feel when you take care of your pet?
- Why is it important to take care of animals in your family?
- What can you do to remember your pet-care responsibilities?

Conclusion: At home, being honest, helpful, and kind makes everyone feel happy and cared for. Whether it is cleaning up, sharing, or admitting a mistake, your actions show that you love and respect your family. Keep practicing these skills, and your home will be full of teamwork, trust, and smiles!

Chapter 4

Community and Kindness

Helping a Neighbor

Your neighbor is carrying a big bag of groceries and looks like they need help. Should you:

1. With your parent's permission, ask if they need help and carry a small bag for them.
2. Keep playing and pretend you did not see them.
3. Wait for someone else to help them.

Explanation: Helping someone in your community, with your parent's permission, is a kind and thoughtful way to show you care. Even small acts of kindness make a big difference.

Follow-Up Questions:
- How do you feel when someone helps you?
- What are other ways you can help your neighbors?
- Why is it important to help people in your community?

Picking Up Litter at the Park

You are playing at the park, and you notice some trash near the swings. Should you:
1. Pick up the trash and throw it away in a nearby bin.
2. Leave the trash because it is not yours.
3. Tell an adult so they can clean it up.

Explanation: Keeping your community clean helps everyone enjoy the park. Taking care of shared spaces shows responsibility and kindness to others.

Follow-Up Questions:
- How does a clean park make everyone feel?
- Why is it important to take care of places where lots of people play?
- What can you do to help keep your community clean?

Sharing at the Library

You are at the library, and there is only one book left about your favorite topic. Another child asks if they can read it, too. Should you:
1. Offer to take turns reading the book.
2. Keep the book to yourself and read it quietly.
3. Put the book back so no one gets it.

Explanation: Sharing with others in your community, like at the library, helps everyone feel included. Taking turns teaches kindness and patience.

Follow-Up Questions:
- How would you feel if someone shared a special book with you?
- What are other ways you can be kind at the library?
- Why is sharing important in community spaces?

Meeting a New Classmate

Your teacher asks everyone to play a game with the new student. They look unsure of the rules. Should you:
1. Help explain the game so they can join in.
2. Play the game without including them.
3. Wait for someone else to help them.

Explanation: Helping someone new understand a game shows kindness and makes them feel part of the group. Being kind to new people can help them adjust and make your classroom a friendlier place.

Follow-Up Questions:
- How do you think the new student feels?
- What is one thing you could do to make them feel more comfortable?
- Why is it important to welcome new people?

Donating Toys or Clothes

Your parent asks if you would like to donate some toys or clothes you do not use anymore to children who need them. Should you:
1. Pick a few items you no longer use and happily donate them.
2. Say no because you do not want to give anything away, as they are yours.
3. Pick items you still want to keep and change your mind.

Explanation: Donating items you no longer use helps people in need and shows generosity. Sharing what you have is a wonderful way to be kind to your community.

Follow-Up Questions:
- How does giving to others make you feel?
- What is something you could donate that might make another child happy?
- Why is it important to help people who need extra support?

Waiting in Line

You are at the community pool waiting to go down the water slide, but someone cuts in front of you. Should you:
1. Politely tell them that it is your turn.
2. Get upset and yell at them.
3. Let them go ahead and hope they do not do it again.

Explanation: Being kind does not mean letting others be unfair, but speaking up politely shows respect for yourself and others. Taking turns is important for everyone to have fun.

Follow-Up Questions:
- How can you kindly remind someone about taking turns?
- Why is it important to be patient when waiting in line?
- What would you do if someone let you go ahead in line?

Conclusion: Kindness is like magic—it makes people feel good and helps everyone enjoy their time together. Whether you are picking up litter, helping someone, or inviting someone to join your group, your actions show you care. Each little act of kindness makes the world a brighter place. Remember, being kind to others can inspire them to do the same. Let us practice kindness every day to make our community happy and strong!

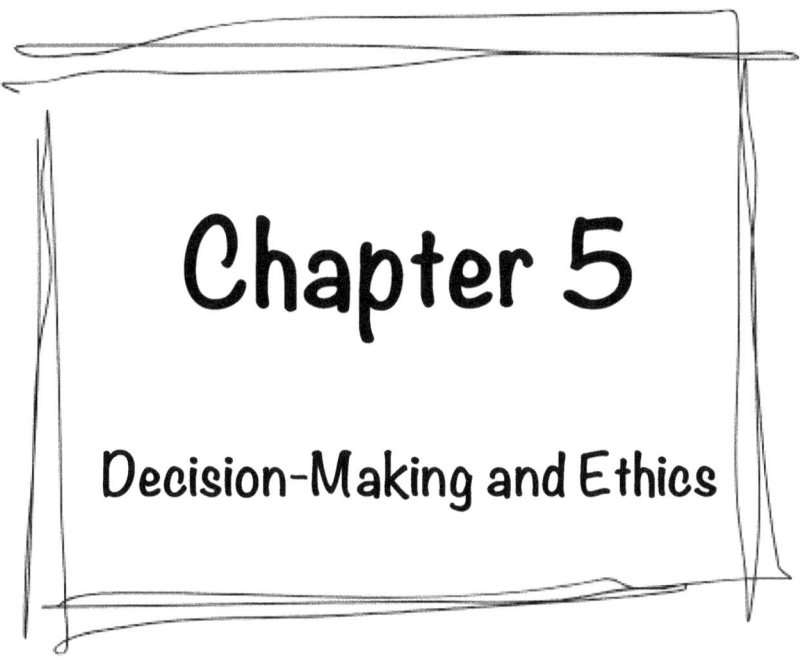

Chapter 5

Decision-Making and Ethics

Finding a Toy at the Playground

You are playing at the playground and find a toy that does not belong to you. Should you:
1. Ask the other nearby children if they lost the toy.
2. Take the toy home because no one seems to be using it.
3. Leave it where you found it in case the owner comes back for it.

Explanation: If something does not belong to you, it is important to try to find the owner or leave it where they might look for it. Being honest helps build trust and fairness.

Follow-Up Questions:
- How would you feel if you lost a toy and someone returned it?
- Why is it important to ask before taking something that is not yours?
- With your parent's permission, what can you do to help someone who lost something?

Breaking a Family Rule

Your parent told you not to eat cookies before dinner, but you see a plate of cookies on the counter. Should you:
1. Wait until after dinner to have a cookie.
2. Sneak one and hope no one notices.
3. Ask your parent if it is okay to have one cookie now.

Explanation: Following rules shows respect and helps build trust with your family. Asking for permission or waiting patiently is the responsible thing to do.

Follow-Up Questions:
- How does following rules show that you care about your family?
- What could you say to your parent if you really want a cookie?
- Why is it important to ask before taking something?

Telling the Truth

You accidentally knock over a vase and it breaks. Your parent asks what happened. Should you:
1. Tell the truth and say you accidentally broke it.
2. Say you do not know who broke it.
3. Blame your sibling or the pet.

Explanation: Telling the truth, even when it is hard, helps others trust you. Everyone makes mistakes, and being honest shows courage and responsibility.

Follow-Up Questions:
- How do you feel when someone tells you the truth?
- What can you do if you make a mistake and feel nervous about admitting it?
- Why is honesty important in your family and friendships?

Picking Teams

You are the leader of a game and get to pick teams. One child who is not as good at the game wants to join your team. Should you:
1. Pick them to make them feel included.
2. Choose only the best players to make sure your team wins.
3. Let someone else pick teams so you do not have to decide.

Explanation: Including others, even if they are not the best at the game, shows kindness and fairness. Making people feel welcome is important.

Follow-Up Questions:
- How do you feel when someone includes you in a game?
- Why is it important to make sure everyone gets to play?
- What can you do to help others feel good about being on your team?

Taking Turns

You and a friend both want to use the same toy truck at the playground. Should you:
1. Set a timer so you can each have a turn.
2. Take the truck and run away with it.
3. Wait quietly until your friend is done using it.

Explanation: Taking turns helps everyone have fun. Using a timer makes it fair and easy to share. Sharing the toy after you are done lets both of you enjoy playing.

Follow-Up Questions:
- How do you feel when someone lets you have a turn?
- Why is taking turns important when playing with others?
- What can you do if you want a turn but someone else is using the toy?

Helping Clean Up

At the end of a playdate, toys are all over the floor, and your friend is about to leave. Should you:
1. Help clean up the toys together before your friend leaves.
2. Let your friend leave and clean up everything by yourself.
3. Leave the mess for someone else to clean later.

Explanation: Helping clean up shows responsibility and respect for shared spaces. Working together makes the job quicker and more fun!

Follow-Up Questions:
- How do you feel when someone helps you clean up?
- Why is it important to clean up after playing?
- What are some ways to make cleaning up more fun?

Conclusion: Making good choices can be tough, but it helps you grow into a strong and kind person. When you are honest, brave, and caring, you inspire others to do the same. Whether it is returning something you found, saying no to peer pressure, or being happy for a friend, every good choice makes a difference. Remember, doing what is right is not always easy, but it is always worth it!

Chapter 6

Environmental Responsibility

The Paper on the Playground

You see a piece of paper blowing around on the playground. Should you:
1. Pick it up and throw it in the trash can nearby.
2. Ignore it because it is not your mess.
3. Watch to see if someone else will clean it up.

Explanation: Picking up trash, even when it is not yours, helps keep your playground clean and safe. Small actions like this make a big difference for the environment.

Follow-Up Questions:
- How does cleaning up litter help animals and people?
- What would you say to encourage others to pick up trash?
- How do you feel when your favorite place is clean and tidy?

Turning Off the Faucet

You are washing your hands and notice the water is still running after you are done. Should you:
1. Turn off the faucet to save water.
2. Leave it running because someone else might use it next.
3. Forget about it and walk away.

Explanation: Turning off the water when you are done helps conserve a valuable resource. Saving water helps plants, animals, and people.

Follow-Up Questions:
- Why is it important to save water?
- What are other ways to save water at home or school?
- How does saving water help the planet?

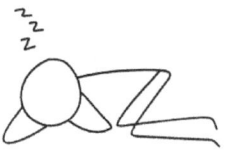

The Broken Crayon

You find a crayon in the art box that is broken in half. Should you:
1. Sharpen the crayon so it is easier to use.
2. Throw it away and get a new crayon.
3. Leave it in the box and use a different color.

Explanation: Using what you have instead of throwing it away helps reduce waste. Being creative with old items is a great way to care for the environment.

Follow-Up Questions:
- How can reusing items help the Earth?
- What is something you can fix or use in a new way instead of throwing it away?
- Why is it fun to come up with creative ways to reuse things?

Planting a Flower

Your class is planting flowers in the school garden, and you are asked to help. Should you:
1. Dig a hole, plant the flower, and water it.
2. Say you do not want to help because it is messy.
3. Watch others plant but not join in.

Explanation: Planting flowers and trees helps make the Earth healthier by giving people and animals food and clean air to breathe. Helping with planting shows care for nature.

Follow-Up Questions:
- How do plants and flowers help the Earth?
- What is your favorite thing about helping in a garden?
- How can planting make your school or neighborhood more beautiful?

Sorting for Recycling

You are cleaning up after a snack at school, and you see a pile of trash with paper, plastic cups, and food scraps all mixed together. What should you do?
1. Sort the trash into the recycling bin, compost bin, and trash can.
2. Ask a teacher if there is a recycling bin nearby.
3. Throw everything in the trash because it is faster.

Explanation: Sorting items for recycling helps keep trash out of landfills and gives materials like paper and plastic a second life. Taking a moment to sort your trash makes a big difference for the planet.

Follow-Up Questions:
- Why is it important to sort your trash and recycling?
- What kinds of things belong in a recycling bin?
- How can you remind others to recycle at home or school?

Turning Off the Lights

You are the last one to leave your playroom at home, and the lights are still on. Should you:
1. Turn off the lights before going into another room.
2. Leave them on because you are not sure if someone else will come back.
3. Wait for an adult to turn them off.

Explanation: Turning off the lights saves energy, which helps the environment. Small actions like this make a big difference in keeping the planet healthy.

Follow-Up Questions:
- Why is it important to save energy?
- What are other ways you can save energy at home or school?
- How does saving energy help people and the planet?

Using Both Sides of the Paper

You are drawing a picture, and the front of your paper is full. Should you:
1. Flip the paper over and use the back.
2. Grab a new sheet of paper for your next drawing.
3. Stop drawing because you do not want to waste paper.

Explanation: Using both sides of the paper helps reduce waste and protect trees. Making small choices like this shows care for the environment.

Follow-Up Questions:
- How does saving paper help trees and animals?
- What are some ways to use less paper?
- Why is it important to think before throwing things away?

Helping the Bees

You notice a bee buzzing near a flower. Your friend wants to swat it away. Should you:
1. Tell your friend that bees help plants grow and leave it alone.
2. Swat at the bee because it is scary.
3. Run away and hope the bee does not follow.

Explanation: Bees are important for pollinating flowers and helping plants to reproduce and grow. Protecting bees shows kindness to nature and helps the environment.

Follow-Up Questions:
- How do bees help the Earth?
- Why is it important to be gentle with animals and insects?
- What can you do to make your yard or garden a friendly place for bees and butterflies?

Conclusion:

The Earth is a beautiful place, and it is our job to take care of it. Whether you are picking up litter, turning off lights, or recycling, you are helping people, animals, and plants live in a cleaner world. Every small action matter, and when you make thoughtful choices, you are helping keep our planet healthy and happy. Show others how much you care about the Earth, and they might join you too! Together, we can make a big difference!

Too Much Screen Time

You have been playing on your tablet for a while, and your parent says it is time to take a break. Should you:
1. Turn off the tablet and play with your toys or read a book.
2. Complain and say, "Just a few more minutes!"
3. Hide the tablet so you can keep playing.

Explanation: Taking breaks from screens helps keep your eyes and brain healthy. Finding other fun activities shows responsibility and creativity.

Follow-Up Questions:
- What are some fun things you can do when you are not using a screen?
- Why is it important to take breaks from technology?
- How do you feel after spending too much time on a device?

Sharing a Tablet

You and your sibling both want to use the family tablet to play games. Should you:
1. Take turns so everyone gets a chance.
2. Grab the tablet and say, "I had it first!"
3. Tell your parent so they can decide who gets to use it.

Explanation: Sharing technology shows kindness and teamwork. Taking turns helps everyone enjoy the fun without arguing.

Follow-Up Questions:
- How can sharing make playtime more fun for everyone?
- Why is it important to be fair when using shared devices?
- What is a good way to take turns without fighting?

Accidentally Clicking an Ad

You are playing a game on your parent's phone and see an ad pop up. Should you:
1. Call your parent and ask for help.
2. Click on the ad to see what happens.
3. Close the app and stop playing.

Explanation: Asking for help when you see something unfamiliar is the safest choice. Ads can sometimes lead to things that are not safe or meant for children.

Follow-Up Questions:
- Why is it important to ask an adult before clicking on something?
- How can you stay safe when using devices?
- What should you do if you see something you do not understand?

Watching a Show with Friends

Your friend wants to watch a show you do not like. Should you:
1. Take turns picking shows so it is fair.
2. Say, "I do not like that show," and refuse to watch.
3. Let your friend pick this time and choose your favorite next time.

Explanation: Taking turns choosing shows helps everyone feel included and happy. Being kind and patient shows good friendship skills.

Follow-Up Questions:
- How does taking turns make watching shows more fun?
- Why is it important to let your friends pick sometimes?
- What is a good way to decide what to watch together?

Goofy Selfies with Family

Your family is having fun taking goofy selfies, and your sibling says they want to go first. Should you:
1. Let them take a few selfies before it is your turn.
2. Say, "No, it's my turn first!"
3. Take a silly selfie with your sibling and then let them have a turn.

Explanation: Sharing the camera and taking turns makes family time more fun for everyone. Including others and being patient helps everyone enjoy the moment.

Follow-Up Questions:
- How can sharing the camera make picture-taking more fun?
- What are some silly poses you can do together to make it more exciting?
- Why is it important to take turns and include others in family activities?

Learning a New App

Your parent shows you a new learning app, but it seems hard to use at first. Should you:
1. Try your best and ask for help if you need it.
2. Say, "I do not want to try this—it is too hard."
3. Close the app and go back to your favorite game.

Explanation: Trying new things helps you learn and grow. Asking for help when needed shows responsibility and a willingness to learn.

Follow-Up Questions:
- Why is it important to try new apps or games that help you learn?
- How can asking for help make learning easier?
- What is something new you learned using technology?

Using Technology Safely

Your friend wants to use your tablet but does not want to follow the rules your parent set. Should you:
1. Tell your friend the rules and make sure they follow them.
2. Let them use the tablet however they want.
3. Take the tablet away and tell your parent.

Explanation: Following the rules when using technology keeps everyone safe. Reminding your friend of the rules shows responsibility and care.

Follow-Up Questions:
- Why is it important to follow rules when using technology?
- How can you explain the rules kindly to a friend?
- What would you do if your friend did not want to follow the rules?

Accidentally Dropping a Device

You accidentally drop a tablet while using it. Should you:
1. Tell your parent right away and apologize.
2. Hide the tablet and hope no one notices.
3. Say it was not your fault and blame someone else.

Explanation: Telling the truth and taking responsibility shows honesty and helps fix the problem. Being careful with devices shows respect for your belongings.

Follow-Up Questions:
- Why is it important to be honest if something breaks?
- How can you be more careful with devices in the future?
- What would you say to a friend who was upset about a broken device?

Conclusion:

Technology can be fun and useful, but it is important to use it wisely and carefully. Whether you are playing games, sharing pictures, or commenting online, your actions should always be kind and thoughtful. Balancing screen time with other activities keeps your mind and body healthy. When you make good choices online, you are creating a safer and happier digital world for everyone. Keep being kind, thoughtful, and responsible, and you will feel great about the way you use technology!

Chapter 8

Emotional Challenges

Feeling Angry

Your sibling knocks over the tower you were building, and you feel really mad. Should you:
1. Take a deep breath and tell them how you feel.
2. Yell at them and push the blocks off the table.
3. Stop building and walk away without saying anything.

Explanation: Feeling angry is normal, but it is important to handle it calmly. Talking about your feelings helps others understand and makes it easier to solve the problem.

Follow-Up Questions:
- How does taking deep breaths help when you feel mad?
- Why is it better to talk about your feelings than to yell and scream?
- What could you say to your sibling to calm the situation?

Missing a Parent

Your parent is away for the day, and you start to miss them. Should you:
1. Draw a picture for them to show when they get back.
2. Cry and say, "I want them back now!"
3. Sit quietly and feel sad without telling anyone.

Explanation: It is okay to miss someone, but doing something kind for them, like drawing a picture, can help you feel better. Talking to another family member about how you feel can also help.

Follow-Up Questions:
- What is a nice way to let someone know you missed them?
- How can talking to someone help when you are feeling sad?
- What other things can you do to feel better when you miss someone?

Feeling Nervous

You are about to meet a new group of children at a playdate, and you feel nervous. Should you:
1. Smile and say hello to someone new.
2. Stay close to your parent and not talk to anyone.
3. Say you do not want to go and stay home.

Explanation: Meeting new people can feel scary, but being brave and saying hello helps you make new friends. Taking small steps, like smiling or introducing yourself, makes it easier to join in.

Follow-Up Questions:
- How does it feel when someone says hello to you?
- What can you do to feel braver when meeting new people?
- What is something fun about making new friends?

Being Disappointed

You wanted to go to the park, but it starts raining. Should you:
1. Find a fun activity to do indoors.
2. Sit by the window and feel upset.
3. Complain and say, "This day is ruined!"

Explanation: Disappointment can be hard, but finding something fun to do instead helps turn the day around. Being flexible shows creativity and a positive attitude.

Follow-Up Questions:
- What is a fun thing you can do when plans change?
- How can being flexible help when things do not go as planned?
- How does finding something fun to do make you feel better?

Feeling Left Out

During a game at recess, your classmates do not include you. Should you:
1. Ask if you can join the game.
2. Sit by yourself and watch them play.
3. Decide not to play with them ever again.

Explanation: Feeling left out can hurt, but being brave and asking to join shows confidence. If they say no, finding something else fun to do helps you stay positive.

Follow-Up Questions:
- How does it feel when someone includes you in a game?
- What can you say to join a group kindly?
- What can you do if the group does not include you?

Being Scared

You hear thunder during a storm, and it makes you feel scared. Should you:
1. Cuddle with a stuffed animal or talk to a parent.
2. Hide under the covers and cry.
3. Run around the house yelling, "I am scared!"

Explanation: Feeling scared is normal, and finding something comforting, like a stuffed animal or a hug, can help. Talking about your fear helps you feel safe.

Follow-Up Questions:
- What helps you feel safe when you are scared?
- Why is talking to someone about your fears helpful?
- What can you do to feel calm during a storm?

Feeling Jealous

Your friend gets a new toy that you really want. Should you:
1. Say, "That is a cool toy!" and ask if you can play with it too.
2. Say, "That is not fair!" and stomp your feet.
3. Stop playing with your friend because you feel jealous.

Explanation: Feeling jealous is okay, but being happy for your friend and asking to share shows kindness and helps your friendship grow.

Follow-Up Questions:
- How does sharing toys make playtime better?
- What can you say to be kind when you feel jealous?
- Why is it important to be happy for your friend?

Feeling Embarrassed

You trip and fall in front of your classmates during gym. Everyone looks at you, and you feel embarrassed. Should you:
1. Laugh it off and say, "Oops, I am okay!"
2. Run out of the room and hide.
3. Get upset and yell, "Stop looking at me!"

Explanation: Everyone makes mistakes, and laughing it off shows confidence. Remember, people forget small moments quickly, so it is okay to move on.

Follow-Up Questions:
- How does laughing at yourself make you feel better?
- What can you say to yourself to feel less embarrassed?
- Why is it okay to make mistakes sometimes?

Conclusion: Big feelings like sadness, frustration, and nervousness can sometimes feel overwhelming, but they are also a normal part of growing up. Learning how to recognize and handle your emotions helps you grow stronger and more confident every day. Whether you are feeling left out, struggling with disappointment, or working through nervousness, you can choose actions that help you feel better and show kindness to yourself and others.

Remember, it is okay to ask for help when you need it. Talking to a trusted adult, taking deep breaths, or finding a quiet moment to think can make a big difference. Every time you face an emotional challenge, you have the chance to learn more about yourself and how to handle different situations.

By practicing patience, empathy, and courage, you can turn tough moments into opportunities to grow. Keep being brave, kind, and understanding—you are doing an amazing job learning how to handle all the feelings that come your way!

Chapter 9

Health and Safety

Wearing a Seatbelt

You are in the car, and your friend says they do not want to wear their seatbelt because it feels uncomfortable. Should you:
1. Say, "It is important to wear a seatbelt to stay safe!" and put yours on.
2. Take off your seatbelt too so your friend does not feel alone.
3. Stay quiet and hope nothing happens.

Explanation: Seatbelts protect us in case of an accident. Wearing your seatbelt, even if others do not, is a smart and safe choice.

Follow-Up Questions:
- Why is it important to always wear a seatbelt?
- How can you encourage others to stay safe too?
- What would you say to someone who does not want to wear theirs?

Crossing the Street

You are walking home with your sibling, and they start to cross the street without waiting for the signal. Should you:
1. Remind them to wait for the signal and cross together.
2. Follow them across the street even though it is not safe.
3. Call out, "Be careful!" and stay on the sidewalk.

Explanation: Waiting for the signal to cross the street helps keep everyone safe. Reminding others to follow safety rules shows responsibility.

Follow-Up Questions:
- Why is it important to wait for the signal before crossing?
- What would you do if someone did not listen to your reminder?
- How can you stay safe while walking home?

Washing Hands

Before snack time, you see your friends eat without washing their hands. Should you:
1. Say, "Let us wash our hands together before eating!"
2. Ignore it and start eating too.
3. Tell your teacher that your friend did not wash their hands.

Explanation: Washing hands helps keep germs away and prevents sickness. Encouraging others to wash up shows kindness and care.

Follow-Up Questions:
- Why is washing your hands before eating important?
- How can you remind your friends to wash their hands without being bossy?
- What other times should you remember to wash your hands?

Stranger Danger

You are at the park, and a stranger offers you a toy and asks if you want to play with them. Should you:
1. Say no and stay close to your parent or guardian.
2. Take the toy and go play with the stranger.
3. Ignore them and walk away.

Explanation: It is important to stay safe by not talking to strangers or accepting things from them without your parent's permission. Staying close to a trusted adult keeps you safe.

Follow-Up Questions:
- Why is it important to follow your parent's rules about strangers?
- What should you do if a stranger talks to you?
- How can staying near a trusted adult help you feel safe?

Playground Safety

You are playing at the playground, and you notice your friend climbing too high on a structure. Should you:
1. Tell them to be careful and play safely.
2. Climb up to join them even though it is dangerous.
3. Walk away and hope they do not fall.

Explanation: Playing safely is important to avoid getting hurt. Reminding your friend to be careful helps everyone have fun without accidents.

Follow-Up Questions:
- How can you play safely at the playground?
- What can you say to your friends to help them stay safe?
- Why is it important to follow playground rules?

Healthy Snacks

You are choosing a snack at home, and your sibling picks a candy bar while you pick an apple. They ask why you did not choose candy too. Should you:
1. Say, "I wanted something healthy!" and enjoy your apple.
2. Change your snack to candy so you match them.
3. Tell them candy is not a good snack and leave it at that.

Explanation: Choosing healthy snacks helps your body grow strong. You do not have to change your choice just because someone else picks something different.

Follow-Up Questions:
- Why is it good to choose healthy snacks?
- How can you help others make healthy choices too?
- What are your favorite healthy snacks?

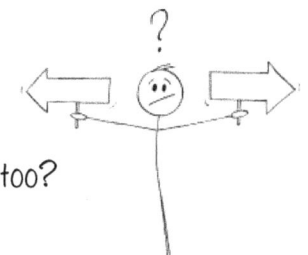

Helmet Safety

You are riding your bike, and your friend says they do not like wearing helmets. Should you:
1. Keep your helmet on and explain why it is important.
2. Take off your helmet so your friend does not feel left out.
3. Tell your friend you will not ride with them unless they wear a helmet.

Explanation: Helmets protect your head from injuries if you fall. Wearing yours sets a good example for others.

Follow-Up Questions:
- How does wearing a helmet keep you safe?
- What would you say to a friend who does not want to wear one?
- Why is it important to follow safety rules, even if others do not?

Fire Safety

At home, you see your sibling playing with matches, or a lighter. Should you:
1. Tell a parent or adult right away.
2. Take the matches or lighter away and hide them.
3. Ignore it and hope they stop on their own.

Explanation: Matches and lighters are not safe for kids to play with. Telling a trusted adult immediately can help prevent accidents and keep everyone safe.

Follow-Up Questions:
- Why are matches, lighters, and fire dangerous?
- What would you say to your sibling about staying safe?
- Who should you tell if you see someone doing something unsafe?

Conclusion: Making safe choices is a big part of growing up. Whether you are deciding to follow a safety rule, avoiding talking to strangers, or remembering to wear your helmet, every choice helps keep you safe. Sometimes, saying "no" or walking away takes courage, but it shows you are smart and responsible. Staying safe does not mean you cannot have fun—it means making good decisions so you can enjoy life safely. Keep practicing healthy habits and staying mindful of your safety, and you will set a great example for everyone around you!

Chapter 10

Cultural Awareness

Different Holidays

Your friend invites you to their house for a holiday you have never celebrated before. They are decorating with bright colors and singing songs in a language you do not know. Should you:

1. Ask them to explain the holiday and join in the fun.
2. Say, "This is weird," and sit to the side.
3. Tell them you do not want to participate because it is different from what you are used to.

Explanation: Learning about other people's traditions is a great way to show kindness and respect. Joining in or asking questions can help you have fun while making your friend feel special.

Follow-Up Questions:
- How would you feel if someone did not want to learn about your holiday?
- What is something new you learned about a different holiday?
- Why is it important to celebrate differences?

Special Clothes

At school, one of your classmates is wearing traditional clothes from their culture for a special day. Some kids are staring at them and whispering. Should you:
1. Tell your classmate their outfit looks beautiful and ask about it.
2. Whisper to your friends that their outfit looks strange.
3. Say nothing and hope no one notices.

Explanation: Complimenting your classmate and asking about their culture shows respect and interest. It helps them feel proud of their traditions and can teach you something new.

Follow-Up Questions:
- How would you feel if someone teased you about your clothes?
- What is a kind way to ask someone about their outfit?
- Why is it important to respect how others dress?

Lunchbox Surprise

Your friend brings food for lunch that looks and smells different from what you are used to. Should you:

1. Ask your friend about their food and say it looks tasty.
2. Make a face and say, "That looks gross!"
3. Ignore your friend's lunch and eat your own food.

Explanation: Being curious about your friend's lunch shows kindness and respect for their culture. Making fun of someone's food might hurt their feelings.

Follow-Up Questions:
- How would you feel if someone teased your lunch?
- What is a kind way to ask about someone's food?
- Why is it fun to learn about foods from different cultures?

A New Song

During music class, your teacher plays a song from another country, and it sounds very different from the songs you usually hear. Should you:
1. Listen carefully and try to sing along.
2. Say, "I do not like this song," and refuse to participate.
3. Giggle and make fun of the music.

Explanation: Music from different places can be fun to listen to and sing. Respecting new sounds helps you learn more about other cultures.

Follow-Up Questions:
- How does music help you learn about different cultures?
- What is something you liked about the song?
- Why is it important to respect other people's music?

A New Game

At recess, a group of classmates invites you to play a game they learned from another country. The rules are different from the games you usually play. Should you:
1. Join in and ask them to teach you the rules.
2. Say, "I only play regular games," and walk away.
3. Watch but refuse to play because it seems too hard.

Explanation: Trying a new game shows that you are open to learning and having fun with others. It also helps you make new friends and learn about their traditions.

Follow-Up Questions:
- What is something fun about learning a new game?
- How can you include others in your favorite games?
- Why is it important to try new activities?

Saying Hello

You visit a friend's house, and their family greets you with a special gesture, like a bow or a handshake. Should you:
1. Try to greet them the same way to show respect.
2. Say, "That is strange," and not greet them at all.
3. Do nothing because you do not know what to do.

Explanation: Learning how other people say hello is a great way to show kindness and respect for their culture. It can also be a fun way to make new connections.

Follow-Up Questions:
- How do you say hello in your family?
- What is a fun or interesting way you have learned to greet someone?
- Why is it important to show respect when meeting someone new?

A Friend's Language

Your classmate speaks another language at home and uses some of those words in class. Should you:
1. Ask them to teach you a word or two.
2. Laugh and say, "That sounds funny!"
3. Ignore them and only talk to those who speak your language.

Explanation: Asking your friend about their language shows interest and respect. Learning a new word can also be fun and help you understand them better.

Follow-Up Questions:
- How does it feel when someone learns a word from your language?
- What is something fun about learning a new language?
- Why is it important to be kind when someone speaks differently?

Conclusion:
The world is full of wonderful traditions, foods, and holidays that make each culture special. Learning about these differences helps us appreciate and respect each other. By being kind, curious, and open, you can help everyone feel included and valued. Even if something feels new or unfamiliar, showing interest shows that you care about your friends and their families. Remember, celebrating differences makes the world more colorful, fun, and full of amazing stories to share!

Chapter 11

Teamwork and Cooperation

Building a Block Tower

Your classmates are building a tall block tower together. One friend excitedly says, "Make it a castle!" while another says, "No, make it a spaceship!" Should you:

1. Suggest combining the ideas to build a castle spaceship.
2. Knock the tower over and say, "Let us start something new."
3. Stop helping and let them argue about what to do.

Explanation: Teamwork means listening to everyone's ideas and finding ways to work together. Combining ideas shows creativity and helps everyone feel included.

Follow-Up Questions:
- How can you make sure everyone gets a chance to share their ideas?
- Why is it important to work together to finish a project?
- How do you feel when others listen to your ideas?

Cleaning Up Toys

During group playtime, everyone is cleaning up toys except one friend who is still playing. Should you:
1. Ask them to help clean up so everyone finishes faster.
2. Tell the teacher they are not helping.
3. Let them keep playing while you do all the work.

Explanation: Teamwork means working together. Nicely asking for help can make cleaning up more fun and faster for everyone. Encouraging others helps build a positive environment.

Follow-Up Questions:
- How does helping each other make things easier?
- Why is it important to clean up as a team?
- What would you say to a friend who does not want to help?

Sharing Art Supplies

During art class, there is only one box of markers for the whole table. One child wants to keep all the blue markers. Should you:
1. Suggest taking turns with the blue markers so everyone gets a chance to use them.
2. Grab the markers you want before they are gone.
3. Use a different color and ignore the child who kept the blue markers.

Explanation: Sharing supplies helps everyone enjoy the activity. Taking turns or suggesting a solution shows teamwork and fairness.

Follow-Up Questions:
- How do you feel when someone shares with you?
- Why is it important to share and take turns?
- What is a kind way to ask for something when someone else has it?

Playing on the Same Team

At recess, you are playing soccer, and one of your teammates keeps missing the ball. Another teammate says, "We should just leave them out." Should you:
1. Encourage your teammate and say, "Keep trying your best!"
2. Agree to leave them out so the team can win.
3. Stop playing and tell the teacher it is not fair.

Explanation: Teamwork means supporting everyone, even if they make mistakes. Encouraging your teammates helps them feel included and try their best.

Follow-Up Questions:
- How would you feel if your team did not include you?
- Why is it important to help everyone feel like part of the team?
- What is a kind way to cheer on your teammates?

Baking Cookies Together

You and your sibling are baking cookies, but they want to mix the dough and add the sprinkles. Should you:
1. Take turns so both of you get to help.
2. Argue over who gets to do what.
3. Let your sibling do everything and not help at all.

Explanation: Sharing tasks and working together makes baking more fun and helps everyone feel included. Taking turns teaches fairness and cooperation.

Follow-Up Questions:
- How can you divide tasks so everyone feels included?
- Why is it more fun to work together than to argue?
- What is your favorite part of working as a team?

Helping a Friend

Your friend is trying to carry a big stack of books but is struggling to hold them all. Should you:
1. Offer to carry some of the books and walk with them.
2. Laugh and say, "That is too many books!"
3. Ignore them because it is not your problem.

Explanation: Helping someone who needs it shows kindness and teamwork. Working together makes the job easier for everyone.

Follow-Up Questions:
- How does it feel when someone helps you?
- What is another way you can help a friend who is struggling?
- Why is teamwork important in everyday situations?

Solving a Puzzle

You and your friends are putting together a big puzzle, but some pieces do not seem to fit. One friend says, "Let's give up." Should you:
1. Suggest trying again and working together to finish it.
2. Say, "It is too hard," and stop helping.
3. Take over and try to do it all by yourself.

Explanation: Solving problems as a team helps build patience and cooperation. Encouraging each other to keep going makes completing the puzzle more rewarding.

Follow-Up Questions:
- How can working together make solving a problem easier?
- What can you say to encourage a friend who wants to give up?
- How do you feel when you finish something as a team?

Painting a Mural

Your class is painting a mural for the school hallway. One classmate keeps painting outside the lines, and another says, "You are ruining it!" Should you:
1. Say, "It is okay, we can fix it together," and help them.
2. Agree that they are ruining it and ask them to stop.
3. Keep painting your part and ignore what is happening.

Explanation: Teamwork means helping others and solving problems together. Being kind and supportive helps everyone feel confident and proud of the project.

Follow-Up Questions:
- How can you help your teammates when they make a mistake?
- Why is kindness important when working on a team?
- What do you enjoy most about working on group projects?

Conclusion: Working together is how teams get things done! Whether it is playing soccer, doing a project, or helping a friend, being part of a team means listening, sharing ideas, and being kind to each other. Cheering each other on, solving problems together, and taking turns as leaders make teamwork fun and fair. Remember, being a good teammate means helping everyone succeed, not just yourself. By practicing teamwork, you will build stronger friendships and make any group you are in even better!

Chapter 12

Imagination and Creativity

Drawing Together

You and your friend are drawing pictures. Your friend says, "Let's draw a jungle full of animals!" but you want to draw a castle with a princess. Should you:
1. Combine your ideas and draw a jungle with a magical castle.
2. Insist on your idea and ignore what your friend wants to draw.
3. Stop drawing and say, "This is too hard to decide."

Explanation: Combining ideas is a fun way to use your imagination and work together. When you share ideas, you can create something even more exciting.

Follow-Up Questions:
- How can mixing ideas make a picture more fun?
- What is a kind way to share your idea with a friend?
- How do you feel when your friend likes your idea?

Pretend Play Adventure

You and your siblings are playing pretend. They want to be astronauts exploring space, and you want to be a pirate sailing the sea. Should you:
1. Pretend to be space pirates who explore new planets.
2. Say your idea is better and play by yourself.
3. Stop playing because you cannot agree.

Explanation: Imagination is more fun when you include others. Finding a way to combine ideas makes pretend play more exciting for everyone.

Follow-Up Questions:
- What is your favorite thing to pretend?
- How can you make sure everyone has fun when playing pretend?
- Why is it important to include your sibling's ideas?

Rainy Day Fun

It is raining outside, and you cannot go to the park. Your parent says, "Let's make up a new game to play indoors." Should you:
1. Use your imagination to create a fun game.
2. Say, "I don't know," and wait for someone else to decide.
3. Complain that staying inside is boring.

Explanation: Rainy days are a great time to be creative. Making up a new game helps turn a boring moment into a fun adventure.

Follow-Up Questions:
- What kind of game would you create for a rainy day?
- How can being creative make boring times more fun?
- Who could you invite to play your new game?

Decorating a Card

Your teacher asks the class to make cards for a holiday. Some classmates are using lots of stickers, while others are drawing pictures. Should you:
1. Use your creativity to decorate your card however you like.
2. Copy exactly what someone else is doing.
3. Say, "I don't know what to make," and leave your card blank.

Explanation: Using your own ideas makes your card special and shows your unique creativity. There is no wrong way to make something with your imagination.

Follow-Up Questions:
- What is your favorite way to decorate a card?
- How can you come up with your own creative ideas?
- How do you feel when someone likes something you made?

Story Time Twist

Your parent is reading you a bedtime story, and they ask, "What happens next?" Should you:
1. Make up a silly or exciting ending to the story.
2. Say, "I do not know," and ask them to finish the story.
3. Say, "I do not want to change the story," and stop listening.

Explanation: Adding your own twist to a story is a fun way to use your imagination. It helps you practice thinking creatively and making stories your own.

Follow-Up Questions:
- What is your favorite part of making up a story?
- How can you make your story exciting or funny?
- Why is it fun to change the ending of a story?

Building with Blocks

You are building with blocks, and you decide to make a tall tower. Your friend says, "Let's turn it into a rocket ship!" Should you:
1. Work together to build a rocket ship with your blocks.
2. Knock down the tower and start over by yourself.
3. Say, "I want to do my idea," and keep building your tower alone.

Explanation: Using your imagination to combine ideas helps make building even more fun. Working together shows teamwork and creativity.

Follow-Up Questions:
- How can you and your friend share ideas while building?
- What is the coolest thing you have ever built with blocks?
- How do you feel when someone adds to your idea?

Costume Creations

You are playing dress-up with a friend, and they find a cape and pretend to be a superhero. You want to wear a crown and pretend to be a king or queen. Should you:
1. Pretend to be a superhero king or queen and save the day together.
2. Say, "You cannot be a superhero," and play separately.
3. Give up and stop playing dress-up.

Explanation: Combining ideas lets you both have fun and create a unique adventure. Imagination is all about exploring new ideas and having fun together.

Follow-Up Questions:
- What is your favorite costume to wear?
- How can you make sure your friend has fun too?
- Why is it exciting to mix pretend play ideas?

Baking Make-Believe

You are playing with your toy kitchen and pretend food. Your friend says, "Let's make pizza," but you want to pretend to bake cookies. Should you:
1. Make a pretend dessert pizza with cookies on top.
2. Tell your friend, "No, we are only making cookies."
3. Say, "This is boring," and stop playing.

Explanation: Imagination makes pretend play more exciting when you find ways to include everyone's ideas. Combining ideas helps you create something fun and unique.

Follow-Up Questions:
- What is the most creative pretend meal you have made?
- How can you share ideas with a friend while playing?
- Why is it fun to try new pretend play ideas?

Conclusion: Your imagination is like a superpower—it makes ordinary moments fun and exciting! Whether you are creating a school project, finding ways to have fun at home, or coming up with new games, your creativity helps you see the world in amazing new ways. Sharing your ideas and working with others makes them even better. Remember, there is no limit to what you can imagine. Keep exploring, creating, and sharing your ideas—you can make every day an adventure!

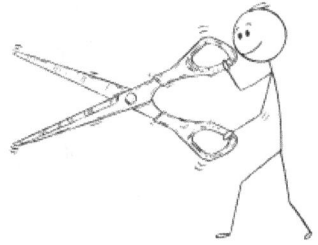

Chapter 13

Responsibility and Independence

Feeding the Dog

Your dog is hungry, but you do not know where their food bowl is. Should you:
1. Look around the house until you find it and feed them.
2. Call for your parent to help and make sure they get fed.
3. Ignore it because it is not your problem.

Explanation: Feeding your pet is an important job. If you need help, asking a parent shows responsibility. Feeding your dog on time helps you show that you can be trusted to follow through with your tasks.

Follow-Up Questions:
- How does feeding your pet help keep them healthy?
- Why is it important to do what you are asked right away?
- How do you feel when you take care of your pet?

Cleaning Up Toys

After playing in your room, your parent says it is time to clean up before dinner. Should you:
1. Start cleaning up right away so you have time to play more later.
2. Say, "I will do it later," and leave the mess.
3. Ask your parent to help clean up so it goes faster.

Explanation: Cleaning up after yourself shows responsibility and keeps your space neat and safe. Doing it on your own helps you practice independence.

Follow-Up Questions:
- Why is cleaning up your toys important?
- How can cleaning up be turned into a fun game?
- How do you feel when your room is tidy?

Picking Out Clothes

Your parent says it is time to get dressed, and they ask you to pick out your clothes for the day. Should you:
1. Choose your clothes and get dressed by yourself.
2. Wait for your parent to pick out your clothes for you.
3. Say, "I do not want to get dressed," and stay in your pajamas.

Explanation: Picking out your clothes helps you practice independence and decision-making. Choosing your outfit shows that you are ready to take care of yourself.

Follow-Up Questions:
- How does choosing your clothes make you feel?
- Why is it important to get ready on time?
- What is your favorite outfit to wear?

Watering the Flowers

Your family has flowers in the garden, and it is your job to water them. You see your favorite cartoon is on TV. Should you:
1. Pause the show and water the flowers.
2. Watch the show and forget to water the flowers.
3. Say, "I do not want to do it today," and let someone else water them.

Explanation: Watering the flowers helps them grow and shows that you are responsible. Completing your tasks on time shows that you can be trusted with important jobs.

Follow-Up Questions:
- How does taking care of plants make you feel?
- Why is it important to finish your tasks before playing?
- What other ways can you help take care of plants?

Remembering Your Backpack

You are getting ready to leave for school, and your parent asks if you packed your backpack. Should you:
1. Double-check your bag to make sure you have everything.
2. Say, "I will check later," but forget to do it.
3. Wait for your parent to pack your bag for you.

Explanation: Taking care of your belongings and packing your own backpack helps you stay organized and shows that you are ready to be responsible for your things.

Follow-Up Questions:
- How can you make sure you do not forget anything for school?
- Why is it important to pack your own bag?
- How do you feel when you are prepared for school?

Brushing Your Teeth

Your parent reminds you that it is time to brush your teeth before bed. Should you:
1. Go to the bathroom and brush your teeth without being asked again.
2. Say, "I will do it later," and forget to brush.
3. Pretend you already brushed so you do not have to do it.

Explanation: Brushing your teeth every day helps keep them healthy and shows that you can take care of yourself. Doing it without being reminded shows independence.

Follow-Up Questions:
- How does brushing your teeth help you stay healthy?
- Why is it important to listen when someone reminds you to do something?
- What helps you remember to take care of yourself?

Sharing Responsibilities

Your parent asks you to help bring groceries into the house. Should you:
1. Help carry the lighter bags to show teamwork.
2. Say, "I do not want to," and let someone else do it.
3. Sit and wait for the groceries to be put away.

Explanation: Helping with family tasks like carrying groceries shows responsibility and teamwork. Doing your part helps everyone get the job done faster.

Follow-Up Questions:
- How does helping with groceries make you feel?
- Why is it important to share responsibilities at home?
- What is another way you can help your family?

Conclusion: Being responsible and independent means taking care of your tasks and helping out when needed. Whether it is taking care of a pet or helping at home, each step shows you are growing up and becoming dependable. Sometimes, it is hard to balance fun with responsibility, but doing your part helps everyone feel happier and more connected. Remember, being independent does not mean doing everything on your own—it means knowing when to take action and when to ask for help. Every time you practice responsibility, you become more capable and confident. Keep up the great work—you are doing amazing!

Chapter 14

Facing Challenges

The Missing Toy

You are playing with your favorite toy, but when it is time to clean up, you cannot find it anywhere. What should you do?
1. Look carefully in all the places you played to find it.
2. Get upset and stop cleaning up.
3. Ask a parent or friend to help you look for it.

Explanation: It is frustrating to lose something you love, but staying calm and looking carefully helps you solve the problem. Asking for help when needed shows responsibility and teamwork. Getting upset does not help you find your toy faster.

Follow-Up Questions:
- How can staying calm help you find what you are looking for?
- What is a good way to ask for help when you need it?
- How do you feel when you finally find something you thought was lost?

Breaking a Crayon

You are coloring a picture, and your favorite crayon breaks in half. What should you do?
1. Keep using the pieces to finish your picture.
2. Get upset and stop coloring.
3. Ask someone if they have another crayon you can use.

Explanation: When something does not go as planned, finding a way to keep going shows creativity and resilience. Asking for help or using what you have teaches problem-solving and keeps the fun going.

Follow-Up Questions:
- How can you stay positive when something does not go as planned?
- What can you learn by finding a new way to solve a problem?
- How do you feel when you finish something, even if it was hard?

The New Playground Equipment

There is a new piece of playground equipment, and everyone seems to know how to use it except you. What should you do?
1. Watch how other kids use it and then give it a try.
2. Ask a friend to show you how to use it.
3. Avoid it and play somewhere else.

Explanation: Trying something new can be scary, but watching or asking for help can make it easier. Avoiding it means missing out on the fun and the chance to learn something new.

Follow-Up Questions:
- How can watching others help you learn something new?
- Why is it okay to ask for help when you are unsure?
- How do you feel when you finally try something new and enjoy it?

The Puzzle Piece Problem

You are working on a puzzle, but one piece does not seem to fit anywhere. What should you do?
1. Take a break and come back to it later.
2. Try to force the piece into a spot.
3. Ask for help to find the right spot.

Explanation: Puzzles can be tricky, but taking a break or asking for help can give you a fresh perspective. Forcing something does not solve the problem and might make it harder to finish the puzzle.

Follow-Up Questions:
- How can taking a break help you solve a problem?
- Why is it important to keep trying, even when it feels hard?
- How do you feel when you finally solve the puzzle?

The Rainy Day Parade

You have been excited for a parade all week, but on the day of the event, it starts raining, and the parade is canceled. What should you do?
1. Find a fun indoor activity to do with your family.
2. Feel upset all day and not try to have fun.
3. Ask if the parade will happen on another day.

Explanation: Sometimes plans change, and it is okay to feel disappointed. Finding a new way to have fun shows resilience, and asking about a future date gives you something to look forward to.

Follow-Up Questions:
- How can you stay positive when plans do not go as expected?
- What are some fun indoor activities you can do on a rainy day?
- How do you feel when you find something fun to do, even if it is different than what you planned?

The Shy Neighbor

Your new neighbor comes to the park but stays by the swings instead of playing with others. Should you:
1. Go over and say, "Do you want to play with us?"
2. Wait for them to come over on their own.
3. Keep playing and pretend you do not see them.

Explanation: Asking someone to join in helps them feel included and brave enough to play with others. Even a small gesture like saying hello can make a big difference for someone who feels nervous.

Follow-Up Questions:
- How would you feel if you were new and someone said hello to you?
- Why is it important to be kind to others, even if they are shy?
- What are other ways you can help a new friend feel welcome?

The Scratched Knee

You are running outside and trip, scratching your knee. It hurts, and you do not know what to do. Should you:
1. Go to an adult and ask for a bandage.
2. Keep playing and ignore the scrape.
3. Sit down and cry until someone notices.

Explanation: Getting hurt is never fun, but asking for help and taking care of yourself shows maturity. Ignoring an injury might make it worse, and waiting for someone else to notice does not solve the problem.

Follow-Up Questions:
- Why is it important to take care of yourself when you get hurt?
- How can asking for help make things better?
- How do you feel when someone helps you feel better?

The Friend Who Shares

Your friend offers you some of their snack, but it is something you have never tried before. What should you do?
1. Try a small bite to see if you like it.
2. Say no thank you and explain that you are not sure about trying new foods.
3. Take the snack but throw it away without eating it.

Explanation: Trying new things can be exciting, but it is okay to say no politely if you are unsure. Being honest and kind shows respect for your friend's gesture.

Follow-Up Questions:
- How can trying new things help you discover what you like?
- Why is it important to be kind, even if you do not want to try something?
- How would you feel if a friend appreciated something you shared?

Conclusion: Facing challenges can feel scary or hard, but every time you try, you get a little stronger. Whether you are feeling sad about losing, solving a hard problem, or doing something that makes you nervous, challenges are chances to learn and grow.

Remember, it is okay to ask for help, take your time, and keep trying. When you face challenges with bravery and a positive attitude, you will be amazed at how much you can do.

Chapter 15

Becoming Your Best Self

The Power of Your Choices

Imagine a day when you made good choices, tried your best, and learned something new. Some moments were easy, some were tricky, and some were difficult, but every choice you made helped you grow stronger and smarter.

Message to the Reader

Every day, you make choices. Some are small, like deciding what to wear or eat. Others are bigger, like helping a friend or trying something new. Every choice is a chance to show kindness, bravery, and creativity.

This book has helped you think about how your choices can make a difference. You have learned about:

- Being kind and including others.
- Trying hard and solving problems.
- Being honest and helpful.
- Staying safe and healthy.
- Facing challenges with courage.

Each time you make a thoughtful choice, you grow into the best version of yourself. It is okay to make mistakes—they help you learn and give you an opportunity to try again.

Activity: A Promise to Yourself

Think about everything you have learned. What is one promise you want to make to yourself about the kind of person you want to be?

I promise to _____

_____

Encouragement for the Future

Your choices do not just help you—they inspire others too! When you choose to be kind, brave, and honest, you make the world a better place.

As you finish this book, remember that you have everything you need to keep growing and learning. Ask questions, try new things, and make choices that show how amazing you are.

Closing Thought

Every day is a new chance to learn, grow, and make good choices. Be curious, be kind, and be yourself. You are ready to do great things!

The End.

50 Bonus Questions:

1. What would you do if a friend accidentally stepped on your picture and crumpled it?
2. How do you make someone laugh when they are feeling sad?
3. What is a fun game you can play with someone new?
4. How can you tell if someone wants to be your friend?
5. What can you do if your friend is talking and you want to say something too?
6. How can you help a classmate who forgot their pencil?
7. What should you do if you do not understand a new game at recess?
8. What can you do if you feel too shy to answer a question in class?
9. How do you know when it is time to be quiet and listen?
10. What can you do to remember where your supplies go?
11. What can you do to help your family get ready in the morning?
12. How can you show your sibling that you care about them?
13. What should you do if you see your parent carrying something heavy?
14. How can you help if your family pet seems scared during a storm?
15. What is something you can do to make dinner more fun for everyone?
16. What can you do to help a neighbor who is raking leaves?
17. How can you be kind to someone who speaks a different language than you?
18. What can you do to help a younger child at the playground?
19. What should you do if you see someone drop their belongings in a store?

20. How can you make someone feel special on their birthday?
21. What should you do if you accidentally take something that does not belong to you?
22. How can you decide what to do when two friends want to play different games?
23. What should you do if you feel like someone is being unfair to you?
24. How can you make a decision when you do not know what the right answer is?
25. What should you do if someone tells you a secret that makes you feel uncomfortable?
26. How can you make less trash when eating snacks at school?
27. What can you do to take care of a tree in your yard or neighborhood?
28. How can you remind someone to recycle without being bossy?
29. What is something you can make out of old boxes or containers?
30. How can you help animals near your home feel safe?
31. What should you do if you see something on a screen that scares you?
32. How can you use a tablet or phone to learn something new?
33. What is a fun way to spend time without using a screen?
34. How can you make sure you are sharing fairly when using a device?
35. What should you do if a friend is playing a game on your tablet that your parent said is not allowed?
36. What can you do if you feel frustrated when something does not work the way you want?
37. How can you help a friend who feels scared about something?
38. What is something you can do if you are feeling really grumpy?
39. How can you let someone know you are feeling nervous?

40. What is a kind thing to say to someone who looks sad?
41. What should you do if your shoes feel too slippery on the playground?
42. How can you stay safe when crossing the street with a grown-up?
43. What should you do if your bike helmet feels uncomfortable?
44. How can you make sure you wash your hands for long enough?
45. What is something you can do to make sure your backpack is not too heavy?
46. How can you learn about a holiday that is different from the one you celebrate?
47. What is a kind way to ask about food that is new to you?
48. How can you show respect for a new song or dance from another country?
49. What should you do if someone makes fun of another child's traditional clothes?
50. What is something nice you can say when you meet someone from a new place?

www.ingramcontent.com/pod-product-compliance
Lightning Source LLC
Chambersburg PA
CBHW071723040426
42446CB00011B/2195